I0817565

XTREME UNDERGROUND MYSTERIES

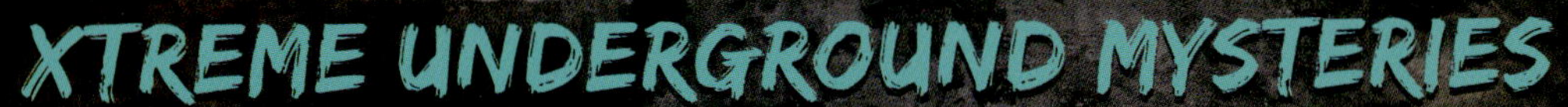

UNDERGROUND CAVES

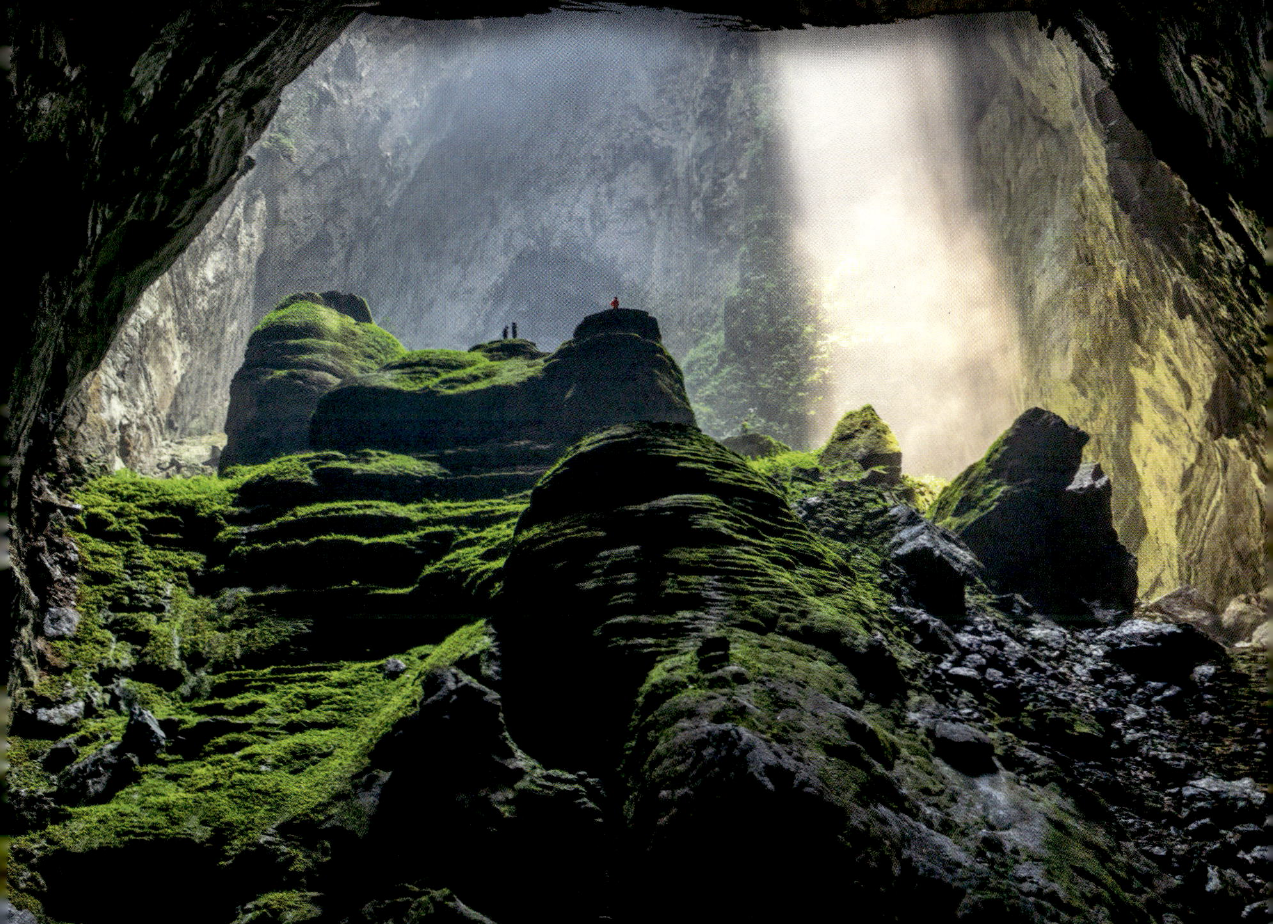

A&D Xtreme
An imprint of Abdo Publishing
abdobooks.com

ANNA ANDERHAGEN

TAKE IT TO THE XTREME!

GET READY FOR AN EXTREME ADVENTURE! THE PAGES OF THIS BOOK WILL TAKE YOU INTO THE WONDROUS WORLD BENEATH YOUR FEET. WHEN YOU HAVE FINISHED READING THIS BOOK, TAKE THE XTREME CHALLENGE ON PAGE 45 ABOUT WHAT YOU'VE LEARNED!

ABDOBOOKS.COM
Published by Abdo Publishing, a division of ABDO, PO Box 398166, Minneapolis, Minnesota 55439.

A&D Xtreme™ is a trademark and logo of Abdo Publishing.
Printed in the United States of America, North Mankato, MN.
102025
012026

Design: Kelly Doudna, Mighty Media, Inc.
Production: Mighty Media, Inc.
Editor: Katherine Chu

Cover Photograph: Janos/Adobe Stock
Interior Photographs: Alexander Van Driessche/Wikimedia Commons, pp. 38–39; Assignment_Houston_One/Wikimedia Commons, pp. 42–43; Charlene Manet/Shutterstock, p. 44; Chip Clark, Smithsonian Institution/Flickr, p. 21; David A Knight/Wikimedia Commons, pp. 10–11; David Kem/NPS Photo, pp. 22–23; Dennis W Donohue/Shutterstock, pp. 20–21; Design Pics/Shutterstock, pp. 26–27; Guy Cowdry/Shutterstock, pp. 36–37; hyunwoong park/Shutterstock, pp. 8–9; Janos/Adobe Stock, p. 1; kid315/Shutterstock, pp. 14–15; Ko Zatu/Shutterstock, pp. 16–17; Lourenço Wilson, Dinh-Sac Pham/Wikimedia Commons, p. 13; Martin Pelanek/Shutterstock, pp. 30–31; Mathias/Adobe Stock, pp. 32–33; NASA/GSFC/METI/ERSDAC/JAROS and U.S./Japan ASTER Science Team, p. 40; NEKOMURA/Shutterstock, pp. 6–7; Newtonian/Shutterstock, pp. 40–41; Petr Lyubimov/Wikimedia Commons, pp. 28–29; Sergei Kazantsev/Wikimedia Commons, pp. 24–25; Shaun Jeffers/Shutterstock, pp. 34–35; Thomas DiGiovannangelo/NPS Photo, pp. 18–19; Uwe Schneehagen/Wikimedia Commons, p. 34; Vietnam Stock Images/Shutterstock, pp. 4–5, 12–13
Design Elements: tsayuet/Adobe Stock (rocky texture); Tunatura/Adobe Stock (tunnel texture)

LIBRARY OF CONGRESS CONTROL NUMBER: 2025939127
PUBLISHER'S CATALOGING-IN-PUBLICATION DATA
Names: Anderhagen, Anna, author.
Title: Underground caves / by Anna Anderhagen
Description: Minneapolis, Minnesota : Abdo Publishing, 2026 | Series: Xtreme underground mysteries | Includes online resources and index.
Identifiers: ISBN 9781098297831 (lib. bdg.) | ISBN 9798384930648 (ebook)
Subjects: LCSH: Caves--Juvenile literature. | Spelunking--Juvenile literature. | Geosciences--Juvenile literature. | Earth sciences--Juvenile literature.
Classification: DDC 551.44--dc23

CONTENTS

HIDDEN CAVES

Local logger Ho Khanh was lost in the jungle in Vietnam. When it started to rain, he took cover under a rocky cliff. He heard rushing water and felt a cold wind. He looked around and saw fog coming out of a large cave entrance. He had found Son Doong Cave!

Ho Khanh discovered Son Doong in 1991. After he left the cave, he couldn't find it again until 2009.

CHAPTER 2

MYSTERIOUS SPACES

The Caves of Drach in Spain are made of four connected caves. This cave system also has a large underground lake known as Lake Martel (*pictured*).

Most caves need water to form. First, rainwater mixes with **carbon dioxide**. This makes the water **acidic**. The acidic water flows into small cracks in limestone. It slowly breaks down the rock. Over thousands of years, this makes the cracks grow into tunnels. Then the tunnels grow and become caves!

SON DOONG CAVE

Son Doong Cave is in central Vietnam. It has a recorded volume of 1.4 billion cubic feet (38.5 million m^3). This makes it the largest cave in the world.

Scientists believe Son Doong formed about three million years ago. It was created when river water wore down limestone along a **fault line**.

Son Doong is more than 656 feet (200 m) high and 492 feet (150 m) wide. It's also more than 5.6 miles (9 km) long.

Son Doong's second doline has a small rainforest where animals such as birds, monkeys, snakes, bats, and more live.

Over time, thin parts of Son Doong's roof caved in. This created two dolines, or **sinkholes**, which let sunlight into some parts of the cave. So, trees and plants in those areas flourished. Some parts of Son Doong even have underground forests, waterfalls, and rivers.

Son Doong also has many dark passageways. Scientists study the animals living in these areas. They learn how animals adapt to dark environments.

Scientists discovered new **species** in Son Doong. These include fish, lizards, snails, scorpions, and more. Many of these species have see-through bodies and no eyes.

Scientists have found more than seven new animal species living in the dark parts of Son Doong.

The *Vietbocap canhi* is a blind Vietnamese scorpion that lives in Son Doong.

In 2019, explorers found an underwater tunnel in Son Doong. It led to Hang Thung, a new cave. Because it's connected to Son Doong, Hang Thung is considered part of that cave system. This connection increased Son Doong's size by 56.5 million cubic feet (1.6 million m³)!

XTREME FACT

Only 1,000 visitors can explore Son Doong each year. This helps preserve its ecosystem.

A tour of Son Doong includes hiking through the surrounding jungle, crossing rivers, and climbing steep rocks and ropes. Visitors also camp in the cave for three nights.

CHAPTER 4

MAMMOTH CAVE

Mammoth Cave is in Kentucky. The cave has at least 420 miles (676 km) of tunnels. It's the world's longest cave system. The Green River shaped the cave out of limestone ten million years ago.

The river water mixes with rare minerals in the ground. It leaves some of the minerals behind as it drips and flows through the cave. This creates interesting **gypsum** shapes and rock formations.

Acidic groundwater dissolved the rock. This made tunnels and underground rivers and created Mammoth Cave.

Visitors can find natural gypsum shapes that look like flowers on some of Mammoth Cave's walls.

People have lived near Mammoth Cave for at least 12,000 years. By 1200 BCE, people were mining **gypsum** with mussel shells. Scientists have found objects such as fiber sandals and gourd bowls in the cave. Ancient carvings, drawings, and writing can also be found along underground cave routes.

The big brown bat is one of many animal species that can be found in Mammoth Cave.

Scientists have explored Mammoth Cave for more than 200 years. They have studied the cave's minerals, **archaeology**, animals, and plants. Scientists have also discovered new **species** there, such as eyeless fish, shrimp, beetles, and spiders.

The Kentucky cave shrimp can only be found in Mammoth Cave. It is eyeless, see-through, and colorless.

XTREME FACT

The temperature in Mammoth Cave is always 54 degrees Fahrenheit (12.2°C). This is because the cave is underground. So, it's not affected by the weather on Earth's surface.

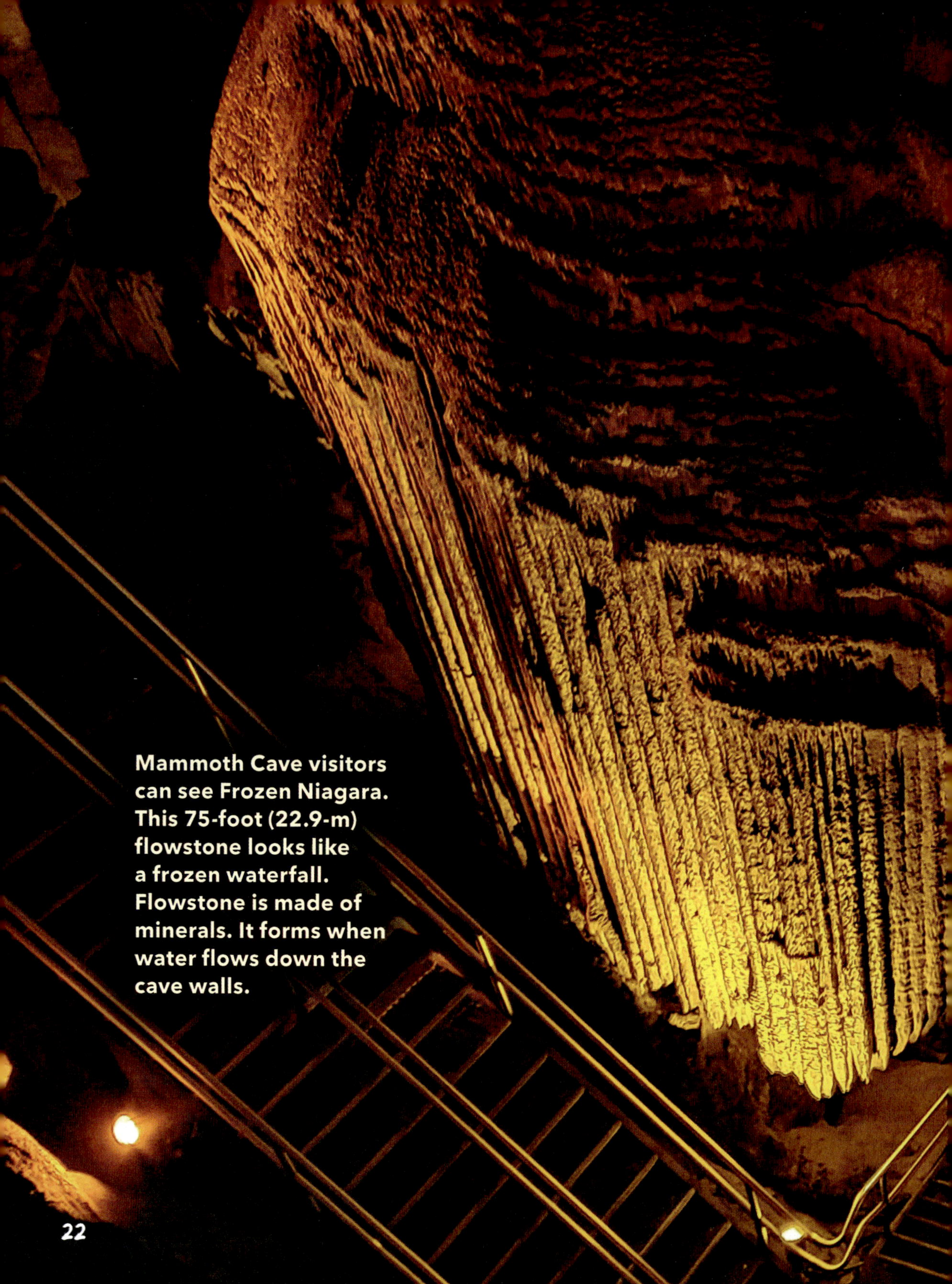

Mammoth Cave visitors can see Frozen Niagara. This 75-foot (22.9-m) flowstone looks like a frozen waterfall. Flowstone is made of minerals. It forms when water flows down the cave walls.

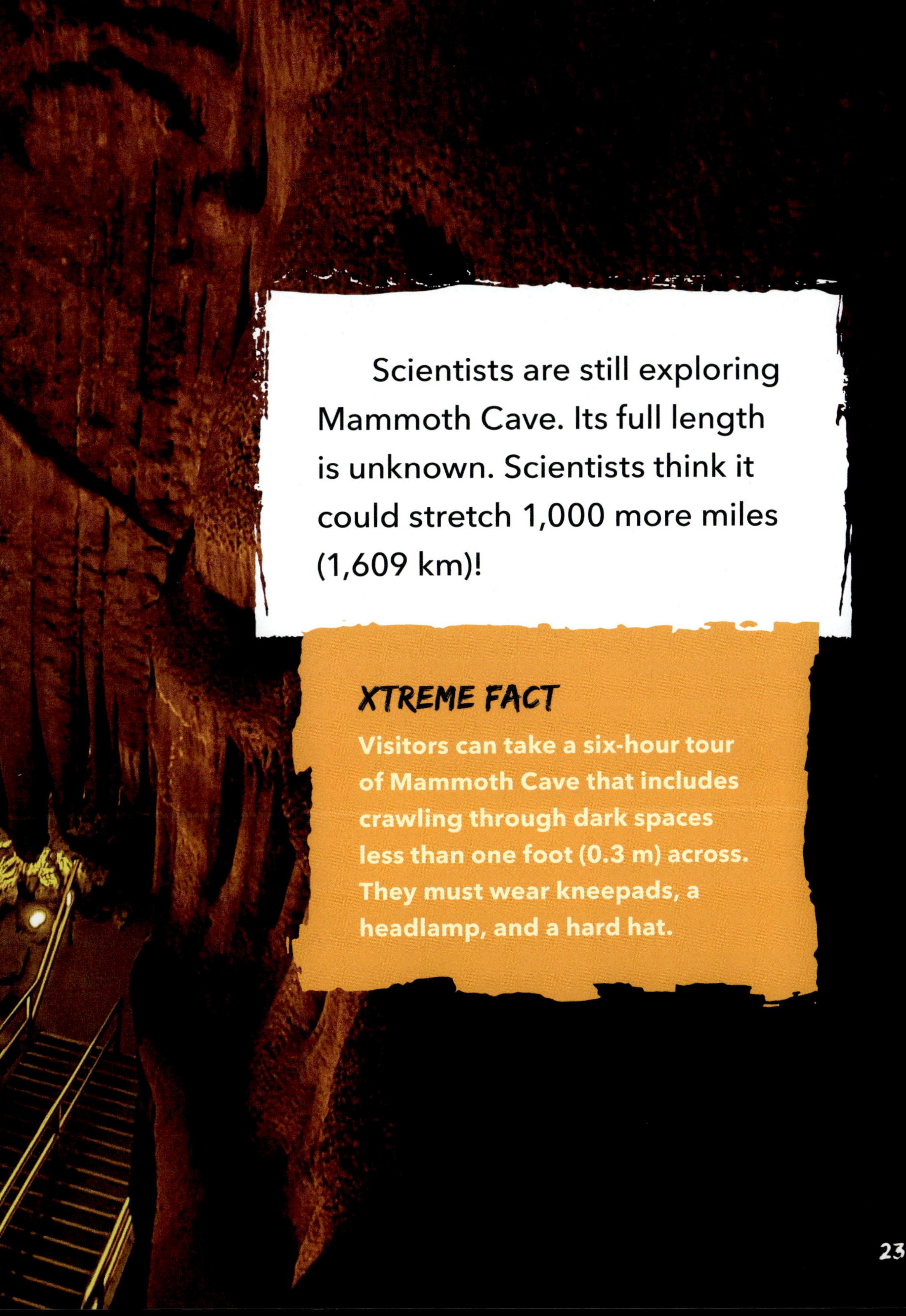

Scientists are still exploring Mammoth Cave. Its full length is unknown. Scientists think it could stretch 1,000 more miles (1,609 km)!

XTREME FACT

Visitors can take a six-hour tour of Mammoth Cave that includes crawling through dark spaces less than one foot (0.3 m) across. They must wear kneepads, a headlamp, and a hard hat.

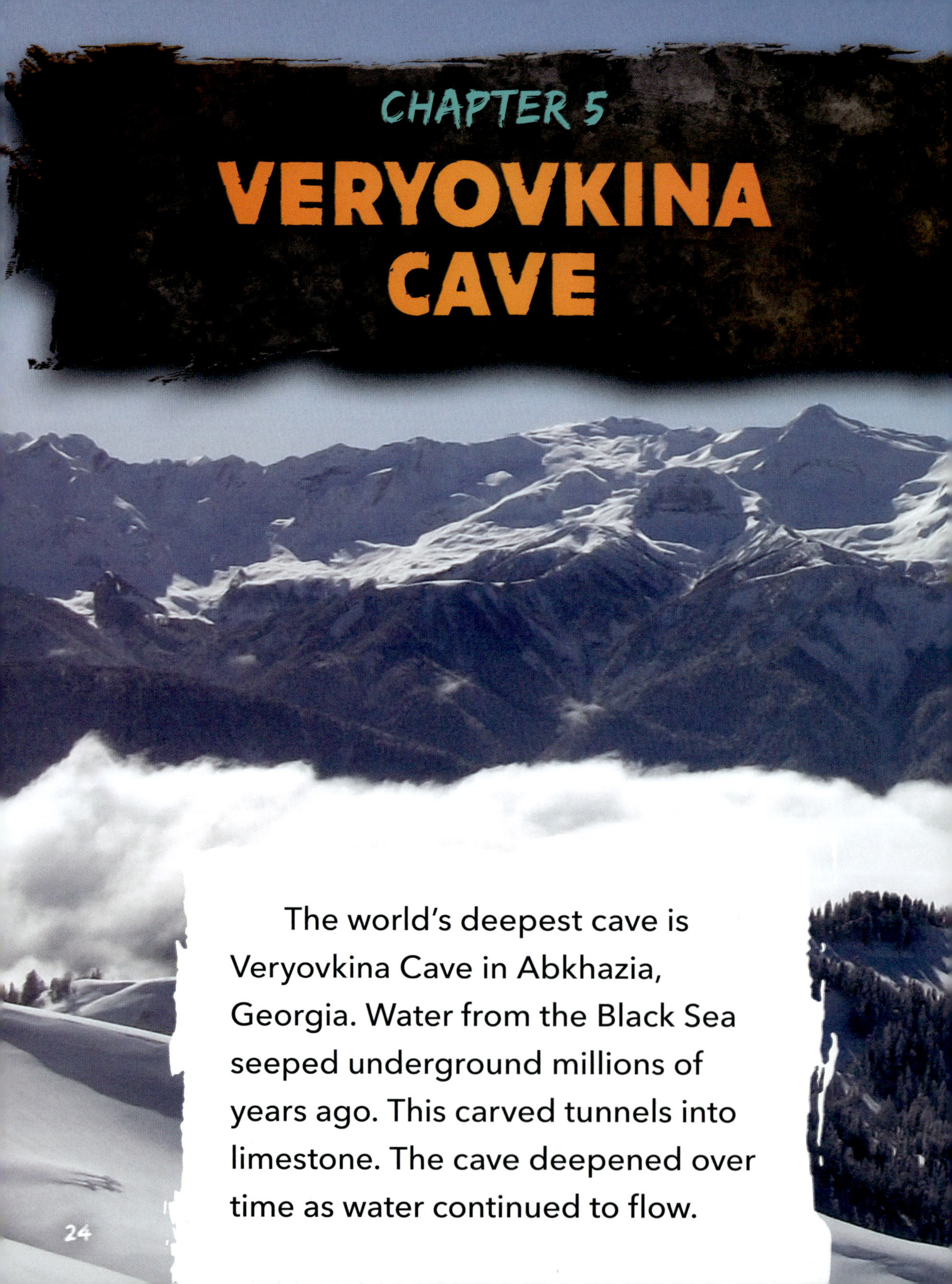

CHAPTER 5

VERYOVKINA CAVE

The world's deepest cave is Veryovkina Cave in Abkhazia, Georgia. Water from the Black Sea seeped underground millions of years ago. This carved tunnels into limestone. The cave deepened over time as water continued to flow.

Veryovkina Cave is in the Arabika Massif (*pictured*). The Arabika Massif is a large area made of limestone in the Gagra mountains.

The Babatunda pit is the biggest pit in Veryovkina Cave.

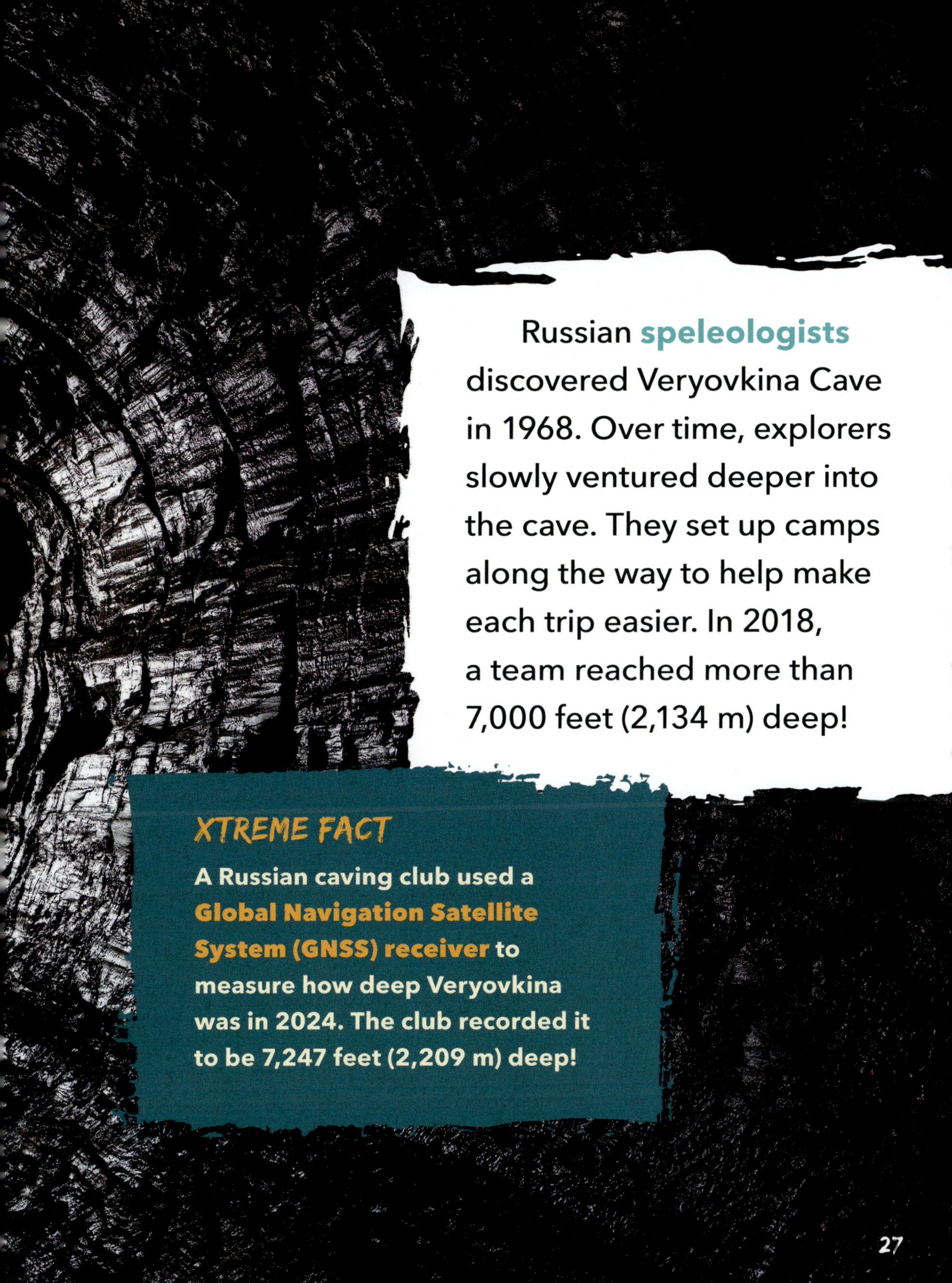

Russian **speleologists** discovered Veryovkina Cave in 1968. Over time, explorers slowly ventured deeper into the cave. They set up camps along the way to help make each trip easier. In 2018, a team reached more than 7,000 feet (2,134 m) deep!

XTREME FACT

A Russian caving club used a Global Navigation Satellite System (GNSS) receiver to measure how deep Veryovkina was in 2024. The club recorded it to be 7,247 feet (2,209 m) deep!

An expedition team member climbs in Veryovkina Cave about 4,593 feet (1,400 m) below Earth's surface.

Speleologists and **geologists** study Veryovkina Cave to learn about Earth's past and unusual **ecosystems**. In 2018, they found rare cave shrimp and scorpions surviving without sunlight. And the cave's rock formations reveal clues about past climates and earthquakes.

CHAPTER 6

THE WAITOMO GLOWWORM CAVES

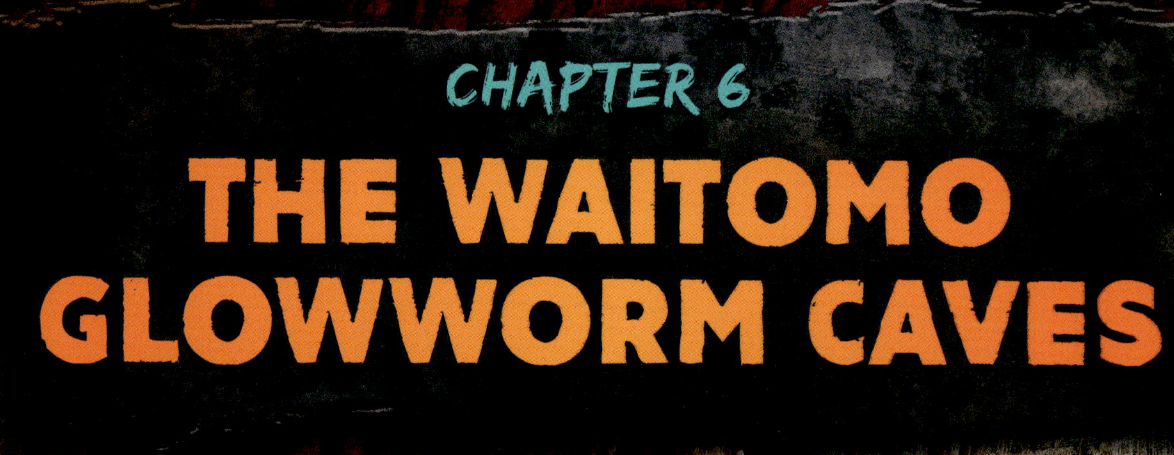

The Waitomo Glowworm Caves are part of the Waitomo cave system in New Zealand. The Waitomo caves are millions of years old. They formed when water wore down limestone. Many of the caves have underground streams that stretch for miles. The streams have created **stalactites**, **stalagmites**, and shafts.

Waitomo is a combination of the Māori words *wai*, which means "water," and *tomo*, which means "sinkhole."

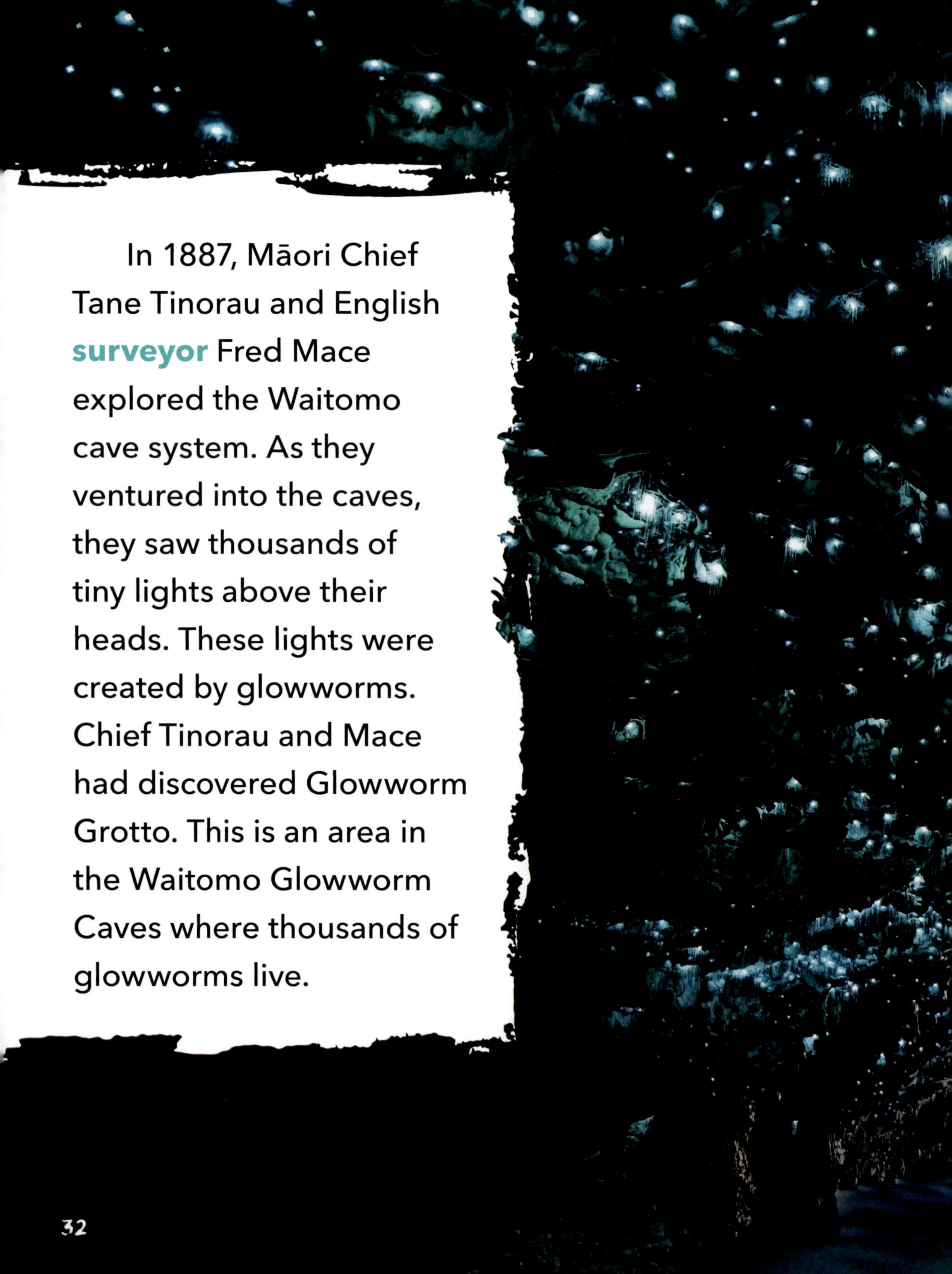

In 1887, Māori Chief Tane Tinorau and English **surveyor** Fred Mace explored the Waitomo cave system. As they ventured into the caves, they saw thousands of tiny lights above their heads. These lights were created by glowworms. Chief Tinorau and Mace had discovered Glowworm Grotto. This is an area in the Waitomo Glowworm Caves where thousands of glowworms live.

The light created by glowworms is called bioluminescence.

XTREME FACT

Local Māori people knew of the Waitomo cave system before Chief Tinorau and Mace's exploration but hadn't fully explored it.

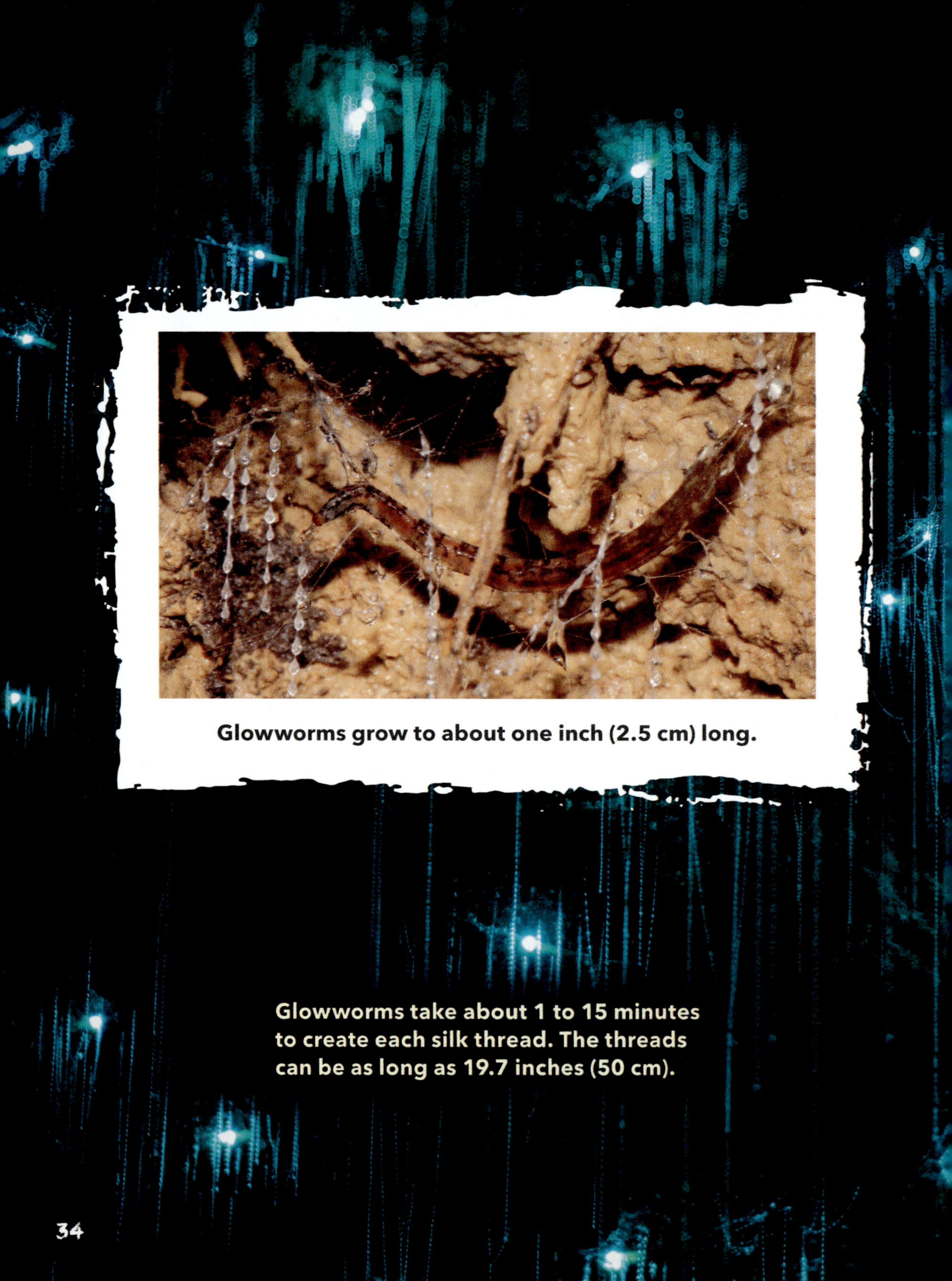

Glowworms grow to about one inch (2.5 cm) long.

Glowworms take about 1 to 15 minutes to create each silk thread. The threads can be as long as 19.7 inches (50 cm).

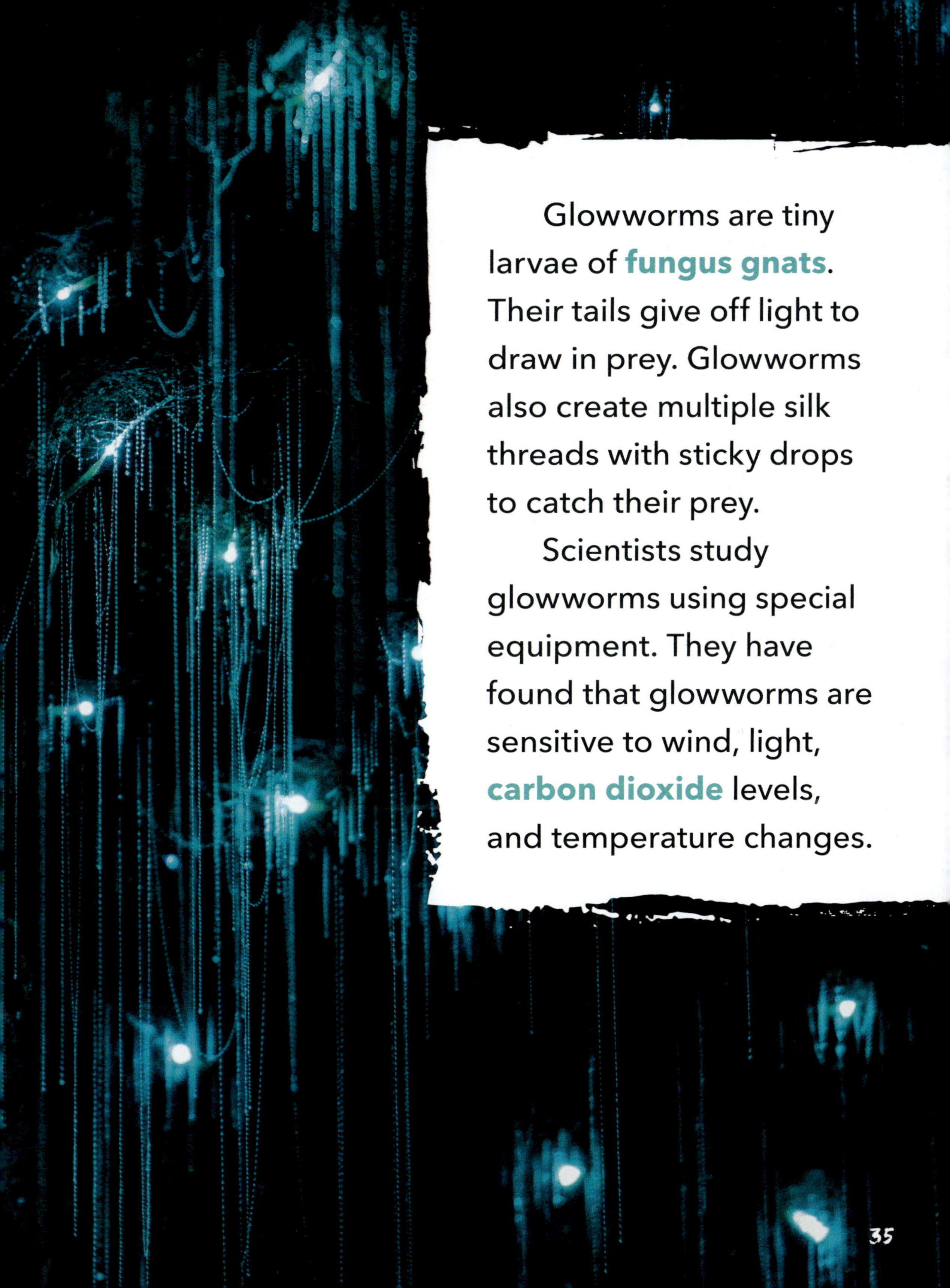

Glowworms are tiny larvae of **fungus gnats**. Their tails give off light to draw in prey. Glowworms also create multiple silk threads with sticky drops to catch their prey.

Scientists study glowworms using special equipment. They have found that glowworms are sensitive to wind, light, **carbon dioxide** levels, and temperature changes.

The New Zealand government took over the Waitomo cave system from Chief Tinorau in 1906. The government did this to protect the caves from damage done by visitors. In 1989, the land was returned to Chief Tinorau's **descendants**. Today, they help maintain the caves and protect the glowworms.

About 500,000 people visit the Waitomo cave system each year.

THE CAVE OF CRYSTALS

Miners discovered the Cave of Crystals in 2000. It's located below the Naica Mine in Mexico. The cave contains some of Earth's largest crystals.

The cave's crystals can be as long as 39 feet (11.8 m). Scientists think the largest crystal weighs about 55 tons (49.9 t).

The Cave of Crystals was found 984 feet (300 m) below Earth's surface.

Because conditions in the Cave of Crystals were so deadly, only scientists with special permits were allowed to enter the cave.

Around 26 million years ago, rising **magma** pushed hot water into limestone. The hot water formed the cave. It also created a mineral layer made of **anhydrite** in the cave.

XTREME FACT

The Cave of Crystals is very hot and has nearly 100 percent humidity. It's risky to stay inside for more than ten minutes without a special suit.

The Cave of Crystals lies in the mountains of southeastern Chihuahua, Mexico.

The hot water slowly cooled over thousands of years. When the water was about 136 degrees Fahrenheit (58°C), the **anhydrite** dissolved into it. This allowed huge **selenite gypsum** crystals to form.

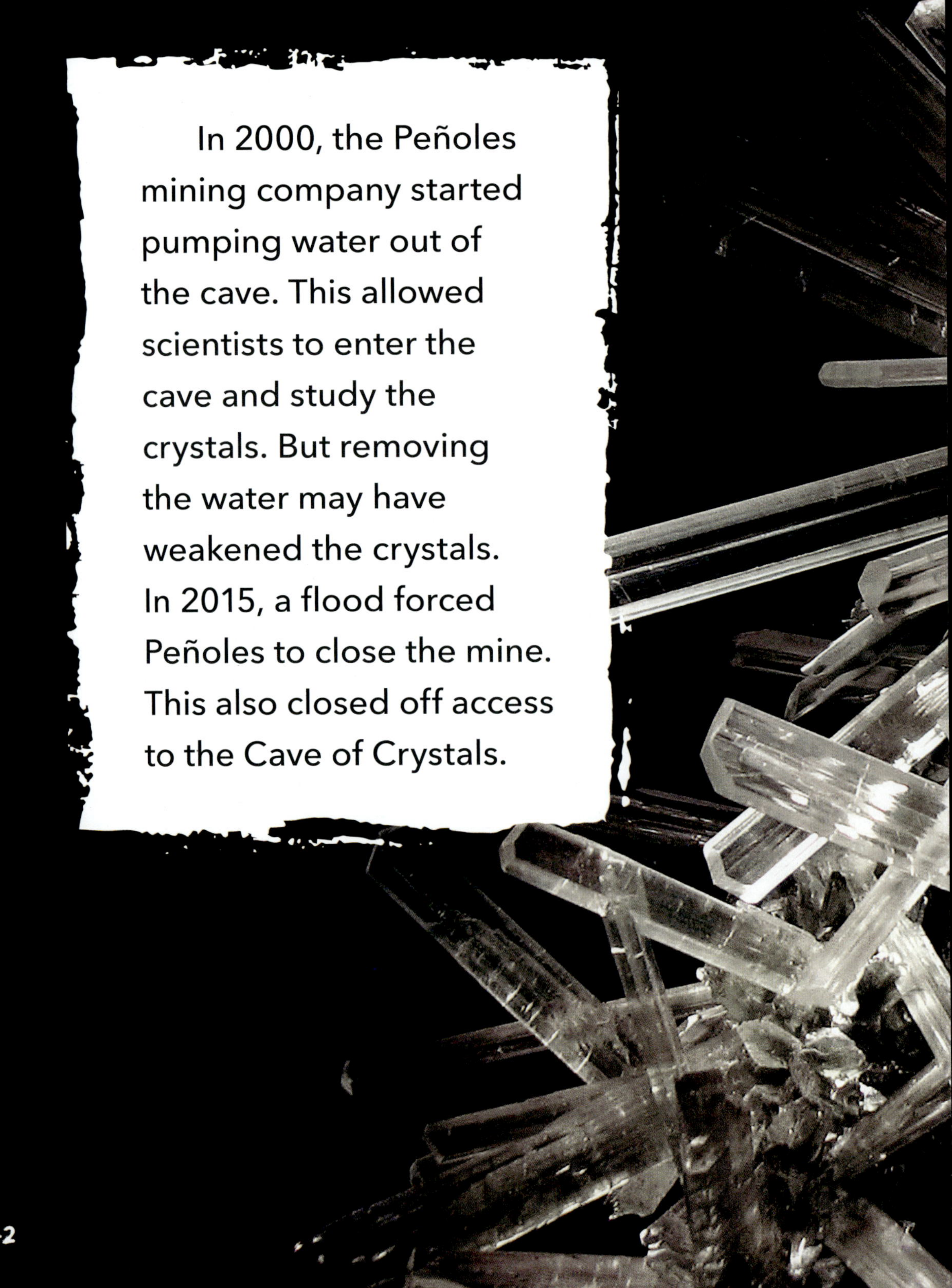

In 2000, the Peñoles mining company started pumping water out of the cave. This allowed scientists to enter the cave and study the crystals. But removing the water may have weakened the crystals. In 2015, a flood forced Peñoles to close the mine. This also closed off access to the Cave of Crystals.

A smaller-sized cave called the Cave of Swords was found in the Naica Mine in 1910. It has crystals that are up to 6.6 feet (2 m) long.

WHAT IS HIDING UNDER YOUR FEET?

Scientists think there may be thousands of undiscovered caves worldwide. And some caves may reach deeper than Veryovkina! The only limit is how far down **acidic** water can seep into limestone. The ground beneath our feet is full of mysteries just waiting to be explored!

Tours of the Waitomo Glowworm Caves include a boat ride through Glowworm Grotto.

XTREME CHALLENGE

TAKE THE QUIZ BELOW AND PUT WHAT YOU'VE LEARNED TO THE TEST!

1) How are most caves formed?

2) If you were exploring a cave, what information would you collect and why?

3) What makes cave animals different from animals that live on the surface?

4) Why do you think protecting caves is important?

GLOSSARY

acidic–containing a type of chemical that reacts when mixed with a base.

anhydrite–dry rock that forms underground and can turn into soft rock called gypsum if it gets wet.

archaeology– the study of the remains of the culture of an ancient people.

carbon dioxide–a heavy, colorless gas that is released when people and animals breathe out and produced when some fuels are burned.

descendant–a person or people belonging to a later generation of the same family.

ecosystem–a community of organisms and their surroundings.

fault line–a break or multiple breaks between two blocks of rock, allowing the rocks to move.

fungus gnat–a type of small fly that eats rotting organic matter.

geologist–a person who studies the science of Earth and its structure.

Global Navigation Satellite System (GNSS) receiver–a device that uses signals from a manufactured object that orbits Earth. The device uses the signals to calculate its exact location.

gypsum–a soft mineral that is naturally found in crystals or a specific type of rock.

humidity–the amount of moisture in the air.

magma–melted rock below Earth's surface.

selenite—a type of gypsum that is naturally found in clear crystals or crystal masses.

sinkhole—a hole that forms in the ground when the surface collapses, often because the ground beneath it has been weakened or eroded.

species—a group of related living beings that can naturally produce offspring with each other.

speleologist—a scientist who studies caves.

stalactite—a pointy rock that hangs down from the roof of a cave.

stalagmite—a pointy rock that sticks up from the floor of a cave.

surveyor—a person who measures a piece of land to determine its shape, area, and boundaries.

ONLINE RESOURCES

To learn more about caves, please visit **abdobooklinks.com** or scan this QR code. These links are routinely monitored and updated to provide the most current information available.

INDEX